for Jo +

DISTRACTION

TACTIC

FLOW

STEVEN LANGSTAFF

THANKS

Thanks to anyone who has received these poems and clapped, or laughed, or gasped – the reactions gave me some self-belief that I'm on the right track.

To the organisers of the fantastic Manchester spoken word scene, in particular *Verbose, Big Words* and *Speak*. Also, a huge thank you to Nigel and the team at the *Words & Music Festival* for giving me such wonderful opportunities.

To Antony Szmierek for being a constant source of encouragement and willing me to do my first spoken word performance.

To my family for always supporting, coming to watch, liking, sharing, and cheering me on.

And to my wife Eve who pushed me to start writing in the first place and gave me the courage to share some words. I've never looked back.

CONTENTS

Civil Twilight

Thick blankets of sky become pin pricked
Losing integrity and ability to hide
Morning creeps to accumulate its identity
Constructing itself by casting off shade

Lingering silence replaced by low hum
To soundtrack this hue of sepia air
Like the opening credits of some squall
Blank canvas superseding noir

Gathering an outfit to wear for the day
Airport run minibus, fox calling it quits
Stars cast aside for snatches of sun
Slumbering trees shake off the abyss

Dawn chorus conducted by morning herself
Curating the mood of the atmosphere
Watercolour streets wake up to prepare
For sparks of ideas to start turning clear

Commuters thread into motorway tapestry
Guttural engine signals suburban activity
Kicking into gear, gearing up for functionality
Dreams unrealised slope back into reality

Bathing in daylight, sun washed streets shine
Stars scared off so the people align
On well-trodden paths, rigid design
I conquered the night, now the day is mine.

Daily Grind

Tram-lined lifestyle lurching onwards
Wednesday clearer in sight
Hump day they call it whilst brewing up
Hunched over unclean mugs and gossip columns
Through Firswood heading towards the airport
Lit up with screens and texting
Squeezed off into rows of suits
Same sandwich in the same bag
Same small talk with the security guard
Commuting in damp trainers to get changed at your desk
Professional shoes hidden amongst wires and cables
Nice weekend? Get up to much?
What you having for your tea?
Repetition robs days of any meaning, the only certainties the deadline and five o'clock
"How are you?" He asks the cleaner
"I'll be alright this time on Friday" comes the usual reply, the usual chuckle, the usual sense of despair
Clock hands creak broken backed towards the next stop
The next hour
Another wasted hour
The tram home is delayed again
He exchanges the weekly eye roll with the woman who he assumes is in sales
There's no spark between them, only frustration
Dreams of escape, no way out
He checks his balance and sighs.

Pieces

The quest for meaning or something, anything
Has landed itself at the creation of the jigsaw
Puzzled they look at a painting in bits
A photograph massacred into bite size morsels
It's ruined they say, not understanding the game
Of frustratingly painstakingly piecing it back
Together stemming the mood of a saturnine Sunday
Piece by maddening, infuriating piece
You must try to gain some clarity
It's perseverance
It's patience
It's resilience
Much like life they said
Yet this fruitless quest for minuscule clues
Piled up in colour-coded Everests
Is unavailing self-infliction to simply pass the time
You had the bigger picture just to rip it all apart
Into wedges of nothing, pursuit of the trivial
To build back up into something whole
Only to find a heart-breaking hole
A chasm which proves nothing yet all
It's perseverance
It's patience
It's pointless
Much like life they said.

Traditions

I've been thinking a lot about the concept of
tradition
The things we do cos we've always done 'em
The things we do just to say we did 'em
Echoes of years in repetition
Midnight mass at Christmas
despite not believing a word
Early doors Friday pint staggered straight from work
even though you've hated the sight of everyone in
the office since 9:01
on Monday morning

But lately it transpires that tradition is toxic
We cling on to meaning 'til we realise we lost it
Of course it's right to remember the dead
But not when prayer turns to bitterness instead
And we look at our past like it's a culmination of bits
And bobs fallen in place like a greatest hits
We see mistakes, wrongs, ills as anomalies
We pray to false gods and erect effigies
Then protect these idols
as they've been there forever
Regardless of when, where, what and whoever
They rode roughshod over,
it was different back then
Vomited old excuse wheeled out time and again.

Small Talk

Sitting with you in the shallow
                     waters of small talk

Is where culturally
                     we are born

The weather a monologue of
                     grave importance

And the traffic a
                     daily slog

We wax lyrical about
                     such trivialities

as game shows and the dog
                     and that new diet, but

in the tiny, inhaled gaps are the
                     shared understandings.

Is it really trivial if we connect?

Village of the Dead
(Village des Morts)

Sun-soaked, dripping in silence
This dead town grips its souls in strips
Row upon row of historic grief
Maps of note, plotted points, details of deceased
We pass down anguished avenues of hurt
Generations of names carved into stone
By generations of families who call heartbreak home
A monument, a monolith, a tribute to never dying
alone
In banks of tranquillity they all stand still
Adorned with flowers, moss
Eroded. Pale.
The sky steals the show, a magnificent pall
Is the warmth from the sun or am I rapt in it all?
Some other couple and another
Walk the same streets of the deceased and hold
hands
In reverence
We turn the corner and negotiate an alley
To emerge wide-eyed at resplendent wings
Encased in glass and lipstick kisses
You cried
Overwhelmed in absence of sound
Or infinite depictions of love
Preached as a dogma, announced a revelation
We leave in shared silence to let thoughts ruminate
Open-mouthed awe a soundless exclamation
A chorus of crows tweets a message from

the Other Side
Of a prophet who parked up on a moonlight drive
We talked of whether he died true to his own spirit
or according to his own daemons
To one of which we've both succumbed
In the 1st, the 3rd and the 7th
Not to mention a pint or two in a bar in the 11th
Submerged in stickers and signatures
Songs and signs and sorrowful sentiments
Needle whispers before the synthesiser starts
Strange Days
Hour hands weigh heavy as we make for the gates
Perfection seems crass as descriptions go
But we stroll in stunned reverie through row upon
row
Fear swells inside me of a mistimed return
As overexposure can cause the memory to blur

Orphan

Don't get me wrong I love the place
But it's no longer home
Myriad changes, a butterfly
From a chrysalis grown

No longer the punchline
Of a poorly conceived joke
A former whipping boy
Populated by under developed folk

The city is vibrant, a beacon of progress
A guitar riff forged by a unique hand
Demographics constantly evolving
Beautiful, insistent rebrand

This place is no longer mine
It long slipped out of my grasp
Now an orphan of a land I still love
An observer, admiring through time lapse

No Change

Regurgitating soundbites
Of the raging ill-informed
Couldn't care less group
Of careless youth
Rolling over to conform

Exercise democratic right
A demon to exorcise
Pointless task
We'll all just bask
In a fallen nation's demise

Bumbling mumbling darling
Picks at the carcass of care
Sold for scrap
Then acid bath
The kids don't have a prayer

In every cry of every man
In every food bank started
The atrocity
Of poverty
We hear the broken-hearted

Remember your decision
With times inevitably tight
Maybe not for you
As you're in the few
But time will be your inspector all right.

Rosetta and Jonah

Jonah would always live
in his wife's shadow
But being with her meant
he was no longer a widow
She was bold, brassy,
She gave him a thrill
Genuine Chanel handbag
Very Nice, not Cheetham Hill
She comes complete
With pristine, preened toy
Poodle in athletic arms
Her pride and joy
Wanted one for years
Since she was a little boy.
Jonah would always live
in his wife's wake
because his previous three lives
were all a mistake
He had loved and lost
and loved again
Even forced himself to feel
and then
He met her.
A fire, a force of nature
Introduced herself as Rosetta
It just so happens souls can meet later
Shrugged off his old skin to date her
Jonah would always live
To worship at her pedestal

On his knees, metaphorically
This life is wonderful
She saunters up the Promenade
With a grace that can't be taught
She placed her bet when she cast her net
It was Jonah's heart she caught
Jonah would always live
For summer months basking in her shade
Get away for an August break,
the Royal Luxembourg awaits
They've really got it made
Jonah would always live
Now he was immortalised
As the doting, smitten husband
Of a bronze bust statuesque bride.

Stone on the Beach

Somehow you attract my attention
Echoing, beating, pulsing, shrieking
And curl yourself into my grip
A curious, crater-faced piece of the world

Smooth edged, discoloured, pock-marked
You've seen time itself, been change
You've seen empires fall and romantic walks
Been tossed aside for made up sport

Then I wonder, were we meant to meet?
Am I part of a club, an elite to have encountered
your cavities, your weather-worn skin?
How many have held you? How many thought
about it?

History held between finger and thumb.
Who else have you met in a twist of fate?
A king? A child? Been carried by a bird?
Out of a million surely an exclusive group

You were special for a beat, a fleeting meeting
Averted my eyes from a summer read
Two products of rock, two children of earth
Interlocked for a minute until I threw you back

The sea put an arm round you and took you in, but you'll wash up
On the shore, I'm sure, to try your luck
With a squealing manifesto to never be thrown
As you're special enough to be taken home.

Acedia

"I don't need no school" he says
"I'm known round here, I'm a king"
A listless boy with less in his head than on his
shirtless frame
He'd found weed and nothingness
And made his excuses long ago

His majesty surveys his golden land
The one his mum works her fingers into stumps to
provide for him
Dad never stuck around, only room for one lion in
this town
A tidy little life in a messy little kingdom

"Don't make the same mistakes I did" he cries with
half pride
At a little sister doomed to follow in his footsteps
Stopped in her tracks by association
"But I do alright" he ends with a smile

Like jacking it in was a noble cause
Like he wanted nothing, as he'd already won it all
Merely existing, on life support
Perpetual toddler with mood swings and all

The ghost of a future girl who'd cop the swings of
his mood

and fall.

"I don't need no school" his highness repeats
Imagined adulation when he speaks
"And it didn't need me" he beams like a toe rag, a
wrong un, a lovable rogue
"Those teachers, man, I ran them ragged, they'll
always remember me"
He reminisces about a time when at least his name
meant something
to somebody.

Love can be...

Love can be sitting looking at phones
in each other's company
Just like reading the Sunday papers
Love can be video games and online quizzes
and getting drunk
Just like asking how your day was
Love can be littered with mistakes and arguments
and sly digs
Just like a heated intellectual discussion
Love can be slouching in t-shirts
and ignoring the gym
Just like becoming depressed
Love can be the most alarming thing
to happen to a human
Just like fatherhood
Love can just be you and me
Doing stuff and enjoying it together
Not what others want it to be.

Saturday, 3pm

We walk from the warmth of the bar in good time
Wrapped in scarves, we herd forwards
Expectation weighs heavy in conversation.
Could we really do it? The year of promotion?
Men huddle and shout obscenities into the ether
Saturday therapy to air swallowed down grievances
A flying tackle, they're getting stuck in, dad provides
the commentary
Nil-nil with three minutes to go
Do we stay and chance the traffic?
Same old City the old saying goes as defeat is sealed
whilst the match gasps for air
Radio waves filled with rage as commitment is called
into question
It really doesn't matter though
Whichever league or the final score
We'll always keep going back
It's not really the football that matters at all
It's spending the time with my dad.

Sorry State

Vote with your mouth, your scorn
Your disbelief
For a world that could be better
But won't. You won't.
You sit bemoaning the state of things
This mess we're in
You're expressing
Views of sanity yet the box you fill
Suggests madness or at least ill will
Clap for the angels whilst stripping em all
Care for the white, the rich, the already cared for.
Scoff in your boys' club
Tell me it's simply not feasible
It's inconceivable
Lie to my face that you don't adore it
He's done it mate, pulled us through
Like a modern-day Churchill
On the front lines
Paid us all to stay in
Tax! Tax! Quick boys-
It'll be us paying!
Asking me if I have a fiver to spare
Whilst billionaires Imagine a world in which we
share.

Emergency Exit

Your sights were set on commercial aircraft
But it turns out you've decided against
a future in the sky to pay your rent
All because your brother laughed.

He said you should be like him
Sit in an office in front of a screen
in a cycle of monotonous routine
Bus, work, meal deal, gym.

Yes, it's true, you'd be awful in the air
You've no charisma, no motivation
There's no room for you in aviation
You probably should look elsewhere.

But to suggest there's more to be had
By sitting in a swivel chair day after day
a weekly regime of dreading Monday
Makes it clear that it's your brother who's mad.

Faded Glamour of the Seaside Town

Once gaudy, these days maudlin
A town in a shroud awaiting its coffin
Though when sun kissed shores allow the landscape to soften
It's worthy of a kiss of life every so often

Pastel shades peel to reveal a mesh
Of fibreglass innards and chipboard flesh
Wear and tear provides a sinister edge
Anthropomorphic smiles turned menacing mess

With a well-placed chip or well-worn scuff
A broken-ribbed pier has had enough
Its heart remains open but the soul is shut
When the sky is bruised over the boarded up

Threadbare winter season landscape
Creates a bleak take on a weekend break
It holds its own time signature this place
Rhythmic tapping of the bucket and spade

A calm yet brooding edge to the sea
Where sticks of rock pass for delicacy
Where worn copper coins still pass for currency
For light up bingo or a teddy grab machine

Spent up on amusements, they never pay out
They're rigged, nowt drops, they've glued the coins
down
No longer a jewel on a coastline crown
Pure faded glamour of the seaside town

Barren floorboards of ballrooms fester
with the rotting carcass of romantic gesture
Yellowing, age-diseased, thumbed love letter
A moribund moon under which he first kissed her

Haunted houses and high-rise flats
Stark shingled beaches and plastic bags
Postcard humour and kiss me quick hats
Promenade packed with pissed up stags

Yet charm hides itself away inside
This husk where land and sea collide

Chip fat lingers, a part of its soul
The town is ancient, but it never gets old.

None the Wiser

I see you pop like a memory
Appearance in mist and smoke
A floater in the eye of recollection
A reminiscence of a person known
You walk past without a lightbulb
No spark of recognition
Pushing aside any shared understanding
Hallucination
of a spirit
A past, but I know you, I've watched you, seen you
unfold
Your perfection a mask for pleasures
Repressed, dampened down for someone you
impressed
At first light, until it dawned on them
You weren't a guarantee
But a bitter coffee scent
Now I'm near you, yet you're none the wiser
A shoulder brushed past by a semi-stranger
You step back into your chat away from the bar
And I take my leave snap back into social shadow
Back to my seat where I must surely await
The ins and outs of Act 2
You'll never know me, but I know all about you.

Job Title?

Digital platformer
Content provider
Algorithm manager
Online footprint negotiator
Customer reacher
Multimedia social influencer
Unqualified political commentator
Fashion blogger
Gaming vlogger
Attention hogger
Celebrity snogger
Upload completer
Prismatic halo ring light user
Home wear hauler
Budget baller
Charity brawler
Sex-line caller
Food grammer
Follow boost scammer
Baby photo spammer
Mindful meme manufacturer
Responsibly sourced cyber dream weaver
Insta-famous ignoramus.

Valentine

Last year I gave you my heart
Cut it right out of my chest
You were confused as yours works fine
The sentiment of my metaphor lost
A vital organ, you said, was "over the top"
For a token of my emotion
We must have listened to different songs
You seemed put off by infinite devotion
Carrying the embarrassment of my gift
You accepted it and walked away
Two days later to my horror and despair
My dying heart in a charity shop window display
The fourteenth of February transformed into
Halloween
As my chest remains prized apart
Blackened like a tar-kissed lung
Orphaned blood spilling from a wasted heart.

The Proletariat Blues

Turned 16
Post-teenage dream
Got the proletariat blues

Cards were marked
Ambitions parked
With your proletariat blues

Lost not found
Gagged and bound
By the proletariat blues

The future slipped
As wings were clipped
On a plane you didn't choose

Missed your chance
To change circumstance
Now your neck is in the noose

You can't refuse
You pay your dues
In offices, in interviews
You play a game you're pre-programmed to lose
Whilst singing the proletariat blues...

Snowflake

Snowflakes are unique and beautiful
Snowflakes are not racist,
though they paint the landscape white.
It's not a fascist statement but it is change.
Snowflakes are not strong, but have
strength enough to fight
Attempting to take outdated views and make
old wrongs right
Snowflake is not an insult.
Each one crystalline perfection
Dancing down to delicately decorate:
A sympathetic renovation of the land.
If only snowflakes came in a spectrum of colours
As I can feel a snow storm coming.

The Cat

The cat doesn't understand acronyms
Or how to set smart targets
But she seems happy enough

The cat isn't worried by fiscal inflation
Or who wins the Bake Off
She's too busy sleeping loads

The cat can't be bothered with chasing promotion
Or shopping around for lower interest rates
She's more concerned with eating

The cat won't get het up about traffic whilst
contributing to it
Or complain that a 16-year-old wasn't enthused to
put her weekly shop through the checkout
She doesn't have cognitive thought

Sometimes I'm really jealous of her.

Trials and Retributions

He cooked you a meal
You said it was 2 star
With its lack of red wine jus
And the vegetables below par

He painted you a landscape
On only your second date
You told him it lacked imagination
Besides you'd prefer a portrait

He wrote you a sonnet
But you told him it was wrong
That he'd missed the point of sonnet form
And every line was overly long

He sculpted you an effigy
Of your favourite internet meme
"Pedestrian at best", you said
Which slightly lowered his self-esteem

He provided a detailed business plan
For your dream start-up restaurant
But you yawned through the solid profit projections
As it's a dream you no longer want

He chartered a flight to an unspoilt land
With you as his only guest
A tropical paradise would be quite nice
But you thought a city break would be best

He hired the Philharmonic Orchestra
To play Happy Birthday to your mother
You told him she'd have liked an original
composition
Rather than a cover

He invited god round for tea
But you said "no, not today"
He harnessed the ability to part the sea
You said it smacked of cliché

He fought the urge to say you were wrong
When you pronounced it "pacifically"
You told him you were testing his grammar
And he'd failed in pedantry

He essentially cured the common cold
The world rejoiced in his name
You said the word "essentially"
Threw major doubts on his claim

He found Shergar, Lord Lucan and his own
sense of worth
Somewhere between here and Leeds
You were at first disparaging
As you never took heed of his needs

He went into space and found life
He brewed a beer that benefited health
He founded a society built on truth
And with that came inexplicable widespread wealth

You scratch around your house alone
Not a drop of scorn to pour
As you wonder what ever happened to
That lad you'd have "settled for"

You scroll on your phone a bit.

Rooftop Riviera

Lobster red, uninterested in conversing
Straight-backed and sweating in a white plastic chair
Body primed for optimum dispersing
Of rays, his opponent don't have a prayer
That's why he's on the roof, he's squaring up to it,
peacocking
He can't be beaten, he knows best
His gaseous adversary's on the ropes rocking
Crimson marbling battle wound across his chest
Sundialling his chair to face up to his enemy
Until sunny boy ducks down behind mountaintops
Technical knockout, Lobster man crabs sideways
and finally
Mutters a craving for food to the wife he forgot
She's been there all along, unnoticed, unspeaking
They just watch the punch-drunk sun becoming
useless
A sparkler in a bucket their fragile, furious retinas
shrieking
He walks to the edge of the afternoon as the sun
makes its excuses
And melts into the horizon.
HE'S WON!
but tomorrow they fight again.

Delusions of Grandeur

Mad, screaming prophet on Market Street,
do you honestly think you're God's mouthpiece?
Judging whilst shouting a ham-fisted attempt
At a sermon, when secretly it's pure contempt
For those with a differing view on creation
Does your church know you offer
own brand salvation?
Peddling misread fire and brimstone
With a fistful of pamphlets and a cheap microphone
You're not the second coming, not even close
To think, this is the Saturday afternoon you chose.

Realistically, this was always about kissing you

Seeing you in that leather jacket
Took me up to space and back
It severed ties and left me in a spin
Juggernaut hours slipped out my grasp
Not usually one for falling fast but
You made yourself at home under my skin.

Our lives were on collision course
Your ray gun lips a magnet force
Brunette vapour trails my only guide
Nirvana t-shirt, leopard print
Eyes with trouble making glint
Relationship cause of death was suicide

Emotions reincarnate
A heart caused to recalibrate
Stand back, stand down, back off, cease and desist
Fired up to give the slip
Her third time on the graveyard shift
Deleted heartbreak from her bucket list

Rushes of imagined clips-
A hastily knocked up manuscript
The scene was set; you in my camera view
Find her and you've got it made
Your heart knew what my eyes betrayed
Realistically, this was always about kissing you.

Promises, Promises

Take me in your arms to quell post-night out
convulsions
Gather up my spilled-out guts from misguided
indulgence
Regrets heaved up in bile and spit, and always in
abundance
Age old skin adorns ageing limbs, my reflection is
revulsion
A reduction of me,
a deflated and sad reproduction of me
A stark sight to behold in the reality
of day
In a way
This is karma, a vengeance, it's balancing books
Like Dorian grasping for youthful looks
Took this day to see the pain I cause
but it won't stop the drinking or the black outs, of
course
Just need to relax, not live on fast forward
It's a marathon not a flat-out sprint as I race you to
last orders
It's awkward
to become a man I didn't sign up for
Wilfully causing myself harm to provoke internal
uproar

And these memories make me see there's a need to
escape from a habit that negatively presents me
I'm affected, my body's infected, I can't recollect it, I
need to correct this
Unfinished, diminished, incomplete, catalectic
It's not fair on us to feel so disconnected
But wait, I can end this, won't try to defend it but
let's just pretend that we've rescued a friendship

Take me in your arms and quash this swelling in my
stomach
Untie this dreaded hate-fuelled knot that's tethered
to my gullet
Reassure my heart once more, scratch my name
from your bullet
For a promise that I'll make a change, cut down on it
or summat.

Dead Star

Creeping realisation that this is it
The dawning truth has caught us unaware
Impossible to carry on like this
Equal victims in crime, no blame to share
As souls detach, leave shadows in their wake
It's no one's fault - it's just the way it goes
Exciting months become years of mistake
A dying star that faded long ago
Pretence more painful than reality
A smoking ember fades to dullest grey
Put this poor thing out of its misery
Cold and festering, rotting and decay
Was dead before we knew it or could see
That everything we had is history.

Death Rattle

She screams blue murder amongst unwashed clothes
Overflowing with rage, swear words spill
From pallid lips like spit
Once proficient on piano, you know
Before the sauce made a ghost of her,
a spirit I suppose

Blue lights again, but never a siren
Silent disco of disregard
She stumbles haphazardly in towelling skin
Slippers like glass, glasses might slip
Bedded in stink of fags and urine

The paramedics don't take her away
Just placate her and abate her need to berate them
A well-known routine down a seemingly quiet street
They'll be back a few times before the boys in black

A curious collection of hangers on
adorn the threshold of that hovel, squalid drinkers
den
Must be barred from all other places so prop each
other up here

Bring your own, your booze, your stories, and sob
away whilst nobody listens
She's too far gone to offer guidance or sympathy
No island of hope inside a sodden old brain

She shouts injustices into the passive night.

Make Do and Mend

The rot set in a good while back
In fact, to ever describe it as healthy would be
hyperbole
They just coexist, him upstairs, her down
Permanently wearing a dressing gown

When he speaks in company, she snorts
Disapproving oinks of disparagement
Drowns him out with 24 carat disdain
Ignoring him, scrolling, you can hear her eyes rolling

Comments about weight and raised eyebrows are
his weapons of choice
She can't breathe without him faking an
earthquaking rumble
Or pretending to be sucked into her void

Col had promised he'd look after her
For worse, for poorer, in sickness
Assurances he lost appetite for pretty early on
She's been no angel either to be fair

Adorned with plasters the marriage has lasted
But with shot knees it limps on in vain
Denise got her kids, Col got his tea on the table
Mutually beneficial slow death

Scratch the surface for grudging respect
For the fact each has stuck it out for this long
His chair in her eye-line, her clothes are a skyline
Stuffing-less, nothingness, all fight is gone

16 years, the itchiest yet but they dig in
Persevere, wait it out, wasting now
Too much to lose, to think about besides they'd
have to sell the house
They're in too far to turn around

How did it come to be like this?
Cemented silence, bricks of contempt
School daze then love fades
When there's no maintenance or care

Hiya love, he's back from work
The moment that her day gets worse
A habitual kiss hits apathetic lips
Her gaze drops to the floor to search for anything
other than small talk

It's Friday so he'll be on his way to the club
his dad and his dad were patrons of
To drink to forget he ever had a wife
While he's out her knotted chest unties.

21:36 to Nantwich

Glottal stop doors
become bottle-necked pores
On the face of it just a journey home
but when in Rome, when in Rome.

Lads enter train stage right
To cap the end of an epic night
All banter and white shirts, spot a girl on her phone
But she's on her stories and wants leaving alone.

Girl on phone adopts a window seat pose
a minute rant about fast fashion clothes
Self-righteous to a fault with her sliced melon snack
Left the train littered with the plastic pack.

Corridor floor packed with vestibule dwellers
collectively clutching Sunday Times Best Sellers
Spines unbroken, narratives undiscovered
back on screen time once they've snapped the
covers.

Middle-aged man in t-shirt and suit
Hair full of gel and covered in Brut
tries to converse with boozed-soaked words
She declines, he mutters about "stuck up birds".

Snap whip crack of an opening can
from antagonistic bloke who can't stand
and his mates laugh whilst taking pics
and his mates point and take the piss.

Cheesy chip smirks painting sinister eyes
Focus fixated on a poor girls thighs
Feeling exposed she switches place
which angers the bloke with the irate face.

She makes her move towards the door
Decided to alight at the station before
Not worth the hassle, the insinuation
"Why dress like that if you don't want attention?!"

"This is Nantwich", recording reveals
a slow screeching scream from the wheels
the station deserted, PM in decline
Beleaguered plod past Samaritan sign.

Perhaps I'll wait for the one that doesn't stop.

To the Moon and Back

They say the moon was a part of earth
Snicked, prised, broken off
Lunar chip off the old block
Sent wandering away in solitudinous spacewalk

A spirit hanging over the world
Like an ancestor residing two branches up
The proud owner of a three-line legacy
Forgotten in the annals of history

A great uncle who served in some far flung war
On your mother's side, and what was his name?
Possibly Tom, but his existence seems secret
though he lives on in your manner and your eyes are
his sequel.

Could we ever reunite? Meld back together?
Instead of this age old dance we insist upon
Orbiting reason, skirting the issue
Of how this special relationship can continue

Millions of years have us drifting apart
You packed up and shipped off ages ago
To be consumed by silence and vacuumed aura
Like a sullen teenage son or daughter.

Spectre

I felt your soft fingers on my forehead
Comforting me in fragmented sleep
You were never here but your spirit is clear
Your soul living on in seven heartbeats

Transported back to your kitchenette
A washing up bowl as a means to clean
My sister ready for a day on road
A flashback, a memory, hallucinatory dream

Years later we'd make jokes about death
No such thing as fear or reality
You on Christmas Day tipsy and giggling
Wearing a cracker hat laying on our settee

They caught up with us, those jokes
Found us in a packed out service
The songs you loved washed over us all
Nourishing a flower plucked away from you

The spectre of your presence a subconscious trick.

Teeth, Hair, Skin

She looks in the mirror
And the smile is returned
Waited for this for two weeks

Since they first got chatting
All butterflies and smirks
Finally the affirmation she seeks

Applies the finishing touches
Awaiting the fun to begin

Brushes her teeth, fixes her hair, polishes skin

She arrives on time to a bar in town
White wine spritzer
In hand

She's looking for love
In a sea of mistrust
And a clutch of one night stands

Compact safety net to check
concealed spot on chin and

Checks her teeth, hair, skin
In he strides,
all confidence, smiles
Makes his way to the bar from the door

Gestures to her that he'll
Top up her drink
Gets the feeling he's done this before

Successfully flirting
And complimenting her

Teeth, hair, skin

The night escapes
In a premature state
Overdone, the sky is dark

To move things on
He suggests they take
A shortcut through the park

They talk compatibility, baby names
Everything like her

Teeth, hair, skin

The path becomes lost
In the seclusion of night
A discarded wheel from a bike

His eyes turn cold
As he grabs a hold
That's when he decides to strike

Broken, bleeding, bruised
She struggles to feel anything like her

Teeth, hair, skin

Life ebbs away
In crimson-saturated grass
Laboured breath slows to devastating stop

Eyes freeze in time
Ravaged, unrecognised
Like the rips in her tights and new top

Final resting place
Next to a dog shit bin, a mass of just

Teeth, hair, skin

An age old cliché
As early next day
Dawn-rise dog walker found her

Tethered and worn
No longer warm
Rope cutting the wrists where he bound her

Horror film expression
Slashed Chelsea grin, bits of

Teeth, hair, skin

Blue lights and sirens
Soundtrack the day
Parents identify

So full of life
Until one fateful night
No hint of a reason why

Cruelty always hand in hand
With victim's next of kin

Teeth, hair, skin
Teeth, hair, skin.

Sleep Paralysis

I'll claim your sleeping limbs as my own
The demon arrogantly said
I'll strap you in and weigh you down
And force my way into your head

A showreel of fears as I press play
Your darkest dreads ignite
Hilariously, you try to get away
You must know you're mine tonight

I stifle your scream with my knee on your throat
You manage a low rumbling gasp
"Don't dare think there's any escape", I gloat
As I tighten the rib cage's clasp

You struggle to breathe and break yourself free
My force on your chest aches further
Blurred between dream and reality
You witness your own murder.

The Author

Steven Langstaff is a Hull-born, Nantwich-based (via Manchester) poet who has been writing and performing for 10 years.

As one half of a comedy sketch double act, Steven earned 5-star reviews at the Edinburgh Festival Fringe (as well as some not-quite-5-star reviews) and wrote and starred in sketches for BBC1's *Dick and Dom's Funny Business*.

An English teacher by trade, Steven grew as a writer and became more interested in spoken word and the use of language within his work, leading to this collection.

In 2019 Steven supported poetry powerhouse Lemn Sissay MBE at the Nantwich Words and Music Festival to a sell-out audience and sold out of his first self-produced pamphlet *Night Terrors*.

ISBN: 9781099152276

Printed in Great Britain
by Amazon